COST CONTROL AND PROJECT SCHEDULING

Two Major Aspects For Project Success

Ifra Publication

CONTENTS

WHAT YOU'LL LEARN

1. Understanding schedule and cost management
2. Tools and techniques for schedule and cost management
3. Identify the inputs to the Estimate Activity Durations process
4. Identify tools and techniques of the Estimate Activity Durations process
5. Recognize the parametric estimating formula
6. Recognize the three-point estimating types
7. Recognize examples of the outputs of the Estimate Activity Durations process
8. Identify the elements of a typical project schedule
9. Recognize the inputs of the Develop Schedule process

ABOUT THE BOOK

This instructor-led Book provides participants with real world tools to manage the complex problems surrounding schedule and cost management. Students will learn a variety of tools and techniques to see what works and what does not in the real world of project management.

The Books discuss the details of the processes required to manage timely completion of the project. It also includes the processes involved in estimating, budgeting and controlling costs so that the project can be completed within the approved budget.

An effective PM needs to learn to lead projects with confidence, develop and meet requirements, and come in on time and within budget. In this Book, Cost Control and Project Scheduling, you will take an in-depth look at how projects are scheduled and budgeted.

First, you will learn how to sequence tasks and understand dependencies. Next, you will determine critical paths and allocate resources. Finally, you will learn to track expenditures, and harness agile methods.

When you are finished with this Book, you will have the knowledge necessary to schedule and budget your own projects, and be ready to continue your learning for the CompTIA Project+ exam.

WHO THIS BOOK IS FOR

1. Anyone interested in learning about project schedule and cost
2. Anyone interested in Project Management
3. Leaders, managers, entrepreneurs, professionals and project workers with or without formal project management training will improve project management skills and knowledge and will be ready to stand for formal certification.

INTRODUCTION

Hi everyone. My name is Ifra, and welcome to my Book, Cost Control and Project Scheduling. I'm the author of Amazon's series of PMP and Business Analysis Books, and now it's my pleasure to help you learn more about project management and prepare for the CompTIA Project+, PK0-004 exam with this third Book in our CompTIA Project+ series.

Earning a CompTIA Project+ certification is a great way to express your interest in project management as a profession, hone your skills, and learn about some of the tools and techniques leaders in the field utilise to find success. Best of all, the only requirement to take the exam and earn the CompTIA Project+ certification is a passion to learn more about project management. Some of the major topics that we'll cover include developing project schedules, implementing Agile methods, and developing project budgets.

By the end of this Book, you'll know how to define and sequence activities, understand how their relationships impact how projects are scheduled, how to find your project's critical path, how to estimate activity durations and costs, how to implement Agile principles in your project environment, and how to use earned value management techniques to quantitatively judge your project's performance. Interest in learning more about project management is the only prerequisite for this Book, though exposure to project environments can certainly help as well.

This Book, and others in the series, can not only help you learn more about project management and prepare for the Project+ exam, but also serve as a great refresher for established project managers and as an opportunity to earn continuing education credit towards certifications like the PMP. I hope you'll join me on this journey to learn more about managing projects and the CompTIA Project+ certification with this Book, Cost Control and Project Scheduling, at Amazon.

DEVELOPING PROJECT SCHEDULES

Hello and welcome. I'm Ifra, and this is Cost Control and Project Scheduling. This is the third Book in a five-Book series built to help prepare you for the CompTIA Project + certification and the PK0-004 exam. Project+ is a great first step towards learning more about project management, whether you're about to embark on managing your first project, or you'd like to gain expertise and apply more structure to projects you're already managing.

This Book and others in the series can also serve as a great tune-up for those looking to earn continuing education credit, to keep existing certifications, like PMP, active. In the last Book, we discussed how project scope is defined and how resources can be managed effectively. We looked at how effective business cases are generated, and how project charters are developed, we learned how to transform business needs into specific requirements that we can implement through project work, and we saw how work breakdown structures are generated and how they represent all of the work that we must do in order to complete projects.

Finally, we also learned how techniques like resource smoothing and resource levelling can help us best manage our resources, especially when we're faced with constraints. This last area of resource management is particularly key to what we'll discuss in this Book, which is broken down into three chapters. We'll start with a comprehensive look at how project schedules are developed. Then, we'll take a few moments to look at Agile project environments and compare and contrast with traditional, predicted ones. After that, we'll look at how lessons we've learned in developing our project schedule can also serve us well in developing our project budget.

In this chapter, we'll first explore what preparatory activities can help set us up for success in creating our project schedule. Then, we'll look at how activities are defined and sequenced and the type of relationships that may exist between various project activities. We'll look at how activities can depend on one another and how this can impact our scheduling decisions. Then, we'll discuss how activity leads and lags can help us better understand how activities relate to one another and see how resource calendars can help us best allocate our resources to our project's work. After that, we'll take a look at bottom-up estimating and the three key estimation techniques and how they can help us to create a more accurate project schedule. Then we'll move on to introducing the critical path and why being able to identify your project's critical path is so, well, critical to your project's success.

We'll next look at the different ways project schedules can be visualised and the benefits different methods have to offer. Finally, we'll introduce two schedule compression techniques that can help ensure that your project stays on track even when challenges arise. As you can see, we're going to cover a lot in this chapter, so let's jump right in.

PREPARING TO SCHEDULE PROJECTS

In order to begin scheduling our project, we need to assemble a variety of key information that's going to be important to creating that comprehensive schedule.

This includes a complete list of all of the activities that need to be completed within our project, a list of the estimates in terms of the duration for each of these activities, any information regarding sequencing and the priority of various activities, information on milestones and baselines that might not only tell us how we're doing on our project and allow us to have more effective and easy control, but also might be directly tied to the funding that we need to continue project work, as well as any dependencies, in other words, any times where a certain activity has to have been completed before project work in other areas can continue.

In addition to assembling this information, there are a number of key questions that we should ask ourselves and ensure that we have the answer to before we go about our scheduling process. First of all, what methodology, approach, and scheduling tools will be used on the project? This could include a variety of different software packages, any sort of norms or regulations that are specific to our organisation, as well as some thought about the type of methodology that we're going to use in our project environment, whether it'll be more predictive or agile in nature, whether we're going to follow an iterative pattern of planning out our work in small phases or some sort of hybrid of these approaches.

What range is acceptable for duration and resource estimates? How accurate do we need to be? And furthermore, will we build our contingencies in at the activity level, at the work package level, at the component level if we're developing a product that can be divided in such a way, or where are those contingencies going to be? Typically on smaller projects, we want to be very well defined in terms of what our estimates might be because there's less overall for us to handle. In larger projects where there might be multiple phases or project work takes place over a long time, it may be difficult to get a high level of accuracy for all of our estimates up front.

And so we may have one standard for accuracy for early provisional estimates and then a tighter required level of accuracy for the estimates that we can create later on in the project once some work has been completed. What unit of measure will we use when talking about our project schedule? Are we going to measure our time in staff hours, in other words, the amount of time that our resources must work on a particular activity? Or will we use a more standard, generalised measure, just as days or weeks, in order to outline how long we expect various activities to take?

This goes hand in hand with the level of accuracy that we'd like to achieve as well because obviously there will be a difference between trying to measure our accuracy down to the minute or hour as opposed to at the day or week level. Furthermore, we need to also consider what units of measure we'll use for our resources. Are we going to measure these in metres or tons or some sort of other regular unit that we can apply to a variety of our different resources? Ensuring that we use common units allows us to more directly compare various tasks and activities within the project.

Next, what links might we have within our project schedule documents to the work breakdown structure, which indicates the scheduling framework and how it should be structured? What other assets may impact our scheduling as well? It's important for all of our documentation to be unified in nature and for them to easily, readily interlink together so that we can pull information from one and directly relate it to another. For example, if we use activity codes within the work breakdown structure, we should refer to those same codes within our schedule so that it's easy to directly tie one task on one document to what we see on our schedule as well.

How do we plan to keep our schedule up to date, and how often are we going to go back and revisit it to ensure that it remains on track? It could be that this is a semi-automated process with the help of some project software tools, but in any case, it's going to be important and, in fact, one of the key roles of a project manager to revisit this regularly and ensure that the project remains on track. Furthermore, what procedures are going to be used for updates and for progress reports? How should various team members report back to us on any challenges they might be facing that could impact our schedule, as well as how they can give us regular updates to allow us to know the status, whether it's on track or not?

Similarly, what level of variation is considered outside of control and therefore in need of some sort of action to take place? It could be based on the level of accuracy that we need for our project. Running a day or two behind is not going to be the end of the world. Or, in some other environments, simply being a couple hours off schedule might not make a big difference. In any case, at some point, a delay becomes too much to handle without addressing it directly, and so understanding where our control thresholds are can ensure that all team members know when it's important to bring any scheduling issues to the attention of the project manager.

Next, what rules for performance measurement might we use, in other words, what sort of earned value techniques, whether it be baselines, percent of activity completed, or other such measures are going to be used in order to gauge how well we are sticking to our schedule and how well we're doing in accomplishing our project's work? Furthermore, how are we going to establish completion percentages? It's rare for any project to have a direct series of 100 identical tasks that allows us to divide it so evenly into a percentage basis. Instead, it can often be difficult to gauge exactly how large a portion of a project any certain activity might be.

And so setting some guidelines, perhaps some milestones along the way, that allow us to roughly estimate how far into our work we've gone will help us to measure performance more effectively moving forward. Finally, how often are we going to issue different reports, and what format will those reports follow when it comes to our schedule control process? It's important to regularly update key stakeholders, such as the project sponsor, on how well we're doing and how well we're sticking to our schedule, but how are we going to go about that? What information do we need to provide to the project sponsor and to other key stakeholders?

The needs of the team itself or various subteams within our project team might differ greatly from those of high-level executives who want to be kept abreast of project progress at a more abstract, high level. Understanding what information is going to be needed and determining how to best communicate that to each stakeholder who needs it can help us communicate effectively while also controlling our schedule.

DEFINING ACTIVITIES

In order to develop our schedule, we need to know exactly what activities need to be completed in order to fulfil our project's objectives. Our work breakdown structure serves as a great starting point in this regard. In some cases, our work packages might have all of the information that we need. However, oftentimes, for the purposes of a work breakdown structure, we're still going to have a variety of associated tasks that can be further decomposed into individual activities for scheduling purposes.

The final result of this process, this final step of decomposition, is an activity list that we can use for scheduling. For example, in the last Book, we looked at a work breakdown structure that looks something like this for an app that was meant to capture photographs and share them on various social networks. If we look within the Twitter Integration area of our Cloud Services category, we see that there would actually be a number of different activities that need to be completed in order for this Twitter Integration work package to be fulfilled.

Some of these activities could include setting up Twitter API access, integrating with operating system sharing functions, scripting the default language we're going to use for tweets and how the URL to our photo or how we're going to attach that photo to that tweet might work, writing code that passes the picture file to a sharing function, whether again it might be embedded within the tweet itself or if we're going to link to our service externally, as well as customising the sharing user interface in order to match the app's user experience to the extent that's allowed by the operating system.

Now the work breakdown structure itself may be constructed before or alongside this activity list. It's important when we begin to define these activities to involve the team members, subject matter experts, and key stakeholders who are going to be most directly involved in implementing these activities and who would also have the greatest knowledge of the specific steps necessary to bring a feature to life. Iterative planning is often useful when we're defining activities because future work might not always be well understood, or it might rely on earlier work to have already been completed before we can lock in that specific list of activities that will be completed.

We should decompose our work as far as we possibly can for now, and then decompose it further later on when more is known in these sorts of situations. Oftentimes, it may be impossible for us to have terribly specific estimates of how long each activity will take until we have that comprehensive activity list, but by decomposing as far as we can, from as early as we can, we're still able to arrive at better estimates that allow our schedule to better represent the scope of our work. Agile environments work similarly to this as well, but that's a topic that we'll cover in more detail in the next chapter.

SEQUENCING ACTIVITIES

When it comes to managing projects, setting the right order of tasks is almost as important as knowing the tasks themselves. That's because oftentimes, activity sequences may be necessary in order for projects to succeed. In other words, we might have to complete some activities before we can move on to completing others. In many other cases, activity sequences might not be mandatory in nature, but would certainly be optimal for various reasons.

Perhaps it would cost less, perhaps we can move forward more quickly. Maybe the risk would be lower because by completing earlier activities we have a better idea of exactly what must be here. It could be that the quality could be higher and so on. In any case, understanding what the sequence of these activities will be is central to our project scheduling, because not only the duration of each activity matters, but also when we can accomplish each of these. Now when we talk about project activities, one thing is always true. There is a predecessor and a successor to that activity. The only two exceptions are for the first and last activities on the project.

The very first one, Of course, would not have a predecessor because we're just getting started. Whereas the very last activity we complete would not have a successor because, well, it's time for project work to come to an end. There are different types of relationships that activities can have with their predecessors and their successors. In a relationship that could be visualised like this where a predecessor is fully finished before a new activity begins, we might define this as a finish-to-start relationship. However, there are others as well. We could find that multiple activities could take place simultaneously, so long as one begins before the other. This is what we would refer to as a start-to-start relationship.

The number of predecessors and successors can also vary by activity. It's not always the case that only one activity might have to come before we begin work on a new one. Oftentimes, we might have to complete three, four, or more tasks, and then we take the finished work from all of those and use them to combine into whatever this new activity might accomplish. The specific relationship of any activity to those before and after it will also be unique. We should not expect the exact same sort of relationship to exist between each activity on our project. Sometimes we might have to wait for a predecessor to be fully completed before we can begin work on a new activity.

In other cases, we might be able to begin right away after a previous activity is commenced. Information on these relationships is key to defining our requirements, as well as to developing our schedule at large. Let's take a little bit of a closer look at some of the logical relationships between activities that can exist.

RELATIONSHIPS BETWEEN ACTIVITIES

One of the most natural relationships between activities is that of the finish-to-start type. In this, a successor activity cannot begin until a predecessor ends. In other words, step 1 has to be completed before step 2 can begin. An example of this sort of activity relationship is that we can't begin to build a house until the foundation for that house has already been laid. A finish-to-finish relationship is also very common in between activities.

Here a successor cannot end until the predecessor ends. In other words, we can't finish step 2 before step 1 comes to a finish. An example of this type of relationship at work could be that we can't submit our app to the app store until we've actually compiled the app. We have to finish all of the work on it and have it ready to go, packaged up, to send off for submission. A start-to-start relationship is also fairly common as well. Here a successor cannot begin until a predecessor has already started. This makes sense.

In other words, step 1 must be started before step 2 can begin. An example of this type of relationship at work would be that you can't inspect products until production has begun. After all, there's nothing there to inspect, so how could we? Of course, we can't begin step 2 until step 1 is underway. Finally, the one that might seem, at first glance, to be the most common is actually by far the least common type of relationship. That is a start-to-finish relationship. Here, we're saying that a successor cannot end until its predecessor starts. The applied logic here is a little bit hard to follow. We are basically saying that step 2 cannot end before step 1 starts. It's difficult to come up with examples for this type of relationship, although it is theoretically possible because it's so rare.

One example might be that we can't finish our second shift of work before the first shift starts. We might find that this is possible, especially in the case of overlapping requirements where we might be talking about two different things taking place much at the same time with one beginning prior to the other. When we talk about these different types of relationships, of which finish to start is the most common and start to finish is the least common, we use a visualisation that looks like what we see to the right. This is known as a precedence diagramming method.

Here we have each of our different activities listed on nodes, in other words, the letters that you see within circles on this diagram. In between each of these, we make a note of what the type of relationship might be. As you can see, between A and B there is a finish-to-start relationship. However, you also see that there are a number of different areas where we have an additional +5 or +10 associated with these. These numbers indicate the days or work periods of lead or lag that are either required or preferred between different steps. We'll talk about leads and lags and how they can help you more effectively manage your project schedule in a few moments, but first let's take a look at a more simple example at length.

If we are, for example, developing our photo sharing application, we might have to first start by acquiring and installing our development tools. From here, it might be possible for us to go on to two different activities, both of which are any finish-to-start relationship. In other words, we have to have acquired and installed the development tools in whole before we can begin to develop the application's home screen and to generate any certificates that are necessary for third-party service integration. From here, we can move on to a variety of other activities.

Here we see that we can begin developing the photo sharing workflow as soon as we have started the process of generating those third-party certificates. We don't have to have completed this activity first, just have started it. On the other hand, until the app's home screen is developed, we don't want to move on into developing the photo sharing workflow itself, so that activity needs to be completed in whole. The same goes for developing the photo capture workflow, which we only want to begin after we know how the user's experience is going to start each time they open the application. From here, we can move on to two other activities.

Once we have finished developing the photo capture workflow, we can begin developing the photo filter and edit processing systems. On the other hand, as soon as we've begun to develop the photo sharing workflow, we can then move on to generating the social media posting templates that we might use. From here, we can see that we might have begun developing the photo filters and editing user experience along the way, but we can't actually finish that process until we have finished developing our editing and processing features that are going to help power that user experience behind the scenes. Once this is complete and once we finish generating those social media posting templates, we are then finally ready to finish our app store submission process.

We might be able to begin filling in some of the details, such as our app name and description, any metadata or pricing information that would be necessary, any information related to what markets our app might be available in. But until we've completed these features, we can't compile the binary that we're going to send off for inspection and for potential publication onto the store. Of course, this is a relatively simple workflow and one that you might disagree with. If you look at the various relationships here and the activities that we're seeking to undertake, you might go about them in an entirely different fashion. That's up to you and your project team to decide upon.

It's incumbent on you as the project manager to seek out information from various stakeholders, experts, and your team members to understand what the relationship between these activities might be and how best they can be sequenced for your project to be completed.

ACTIVITY DEPENDENCIES

When we sequence our activities and determine the logical relationships between each of them, that may or may not have to do directly with different activity dependencies. Activity dependencies are ways that activities depend on one or more factors in order for them to be started or finished. These dependencies may be either mandatory or discretionary in nature and also either internal or external to the project environment.

Mandatory dependencies may be required by either a law or contract. It could be that if we're developing this project on behalf of a client, that we've agreed to do certain activities in a certain order, especially if that's going to be directly tied to our funding in some sort of way. They may also be required by the nature of the project's work. It may be impossible, just logically speaking, to accomplish certain activities until preceding ones have already been completed. Mandatory dependencies are also known as hard logic, and other sequences are not possible when mandatory dependencies exist.

On the other hand, discretionary dependencies may arise based on either best practices or when we've determined that a certain sequence is desirable. Perhaps it's because we have some resources that are inactive right now that can be applied toward a certain activity, but it could be that that could be tackled by someone else later down the road or perhaps even earlier in the project environment. We've just decided that this particular relationship seems optimal for some reason. Discretionary dependencies are also known as soft logic.

In these cases, other sequences are possible, although we prefer to use a certain sequence for some sort of reason. Internal dependencies involve relationships between project activities. Generally, these are under the control of the project management team. External dependencies, on the other hand, involve relationships between project and non-project teams. Generally, these are not under the control of the project management team. These can be areas where we're working with a client or with another service provider within our organisation at large that's not directly associated with the project or any time that we have to act outside the borders or purview of our direct project team.

An example of a mandatory internal dependency can be the need to publish a software beta before analysing feedback from a testing group. In this case, we are developing the software beta ourselves, and we are going to analyse the feedback that we collect ourselves from the testing group that we've also compiled on our own. However, we simply cannot get this feedback until we have some software for the group to test. In the case of a discretionary internal dependency, an example might be waiting to announce a product until development is complete.

We might prefer this for a variety of reasons, but it might also be possible, if necessary, to announce our product prior to its development being completed, especially after a certain state where we might be putting on some finishing touches, but the general concept is ready for consumption by someone outside the project team, whether it be the public at large or simply other key stakeholders within the organisation. An example of a mandatory external dependency is that we can't begin building a building before a permit is approved by whatever sort of government or regulatory source might be necessary in this case.

Here, we can't directly impact what that permitting process looks like. That's outside the purview of our project team, but it is just as essential as it might have been to create the software beta before testing with our mandatory internal dependency. Finally, another example of a discretionary external dependency would be landscaping after all construction is complete, which would help to eliminate any rework that would be necessary on a new building that we might be constructing. Of course, it would be possible, if necessary, to go ahead and lay down sod, plant trees and flowers, and generally fix up the exterior of our new property prior to everything being completed on the inside.

However, if we have to drive additional trucks onto that grass that we've laid down or perhaps carry in additional materials that could potentially damage any of the trees or shrubs or greenery that we put down, there might be a need to go back and fix this after the fact, and so we would prefer that we wait until our internal work is complete prior to working on that landscaping.

LEADS AND LAGS

When looking at the example of a precedence network diagram a few moments ago, we saw that different activities can be connected to one another and that we state what type of relationship there might be between these different areas. However, we could also add a number to each of these. For example, FF +10 or FS -5, what exactly do these mean?

Well, a lead is the amount of time that an activity may be moved up in a schedule. This allows work to begin closer to or alongside a preceding activity. A lag, on the other hand, is the amount of time that must pass until a successor activity may begin. Leading activities are only possible on finish-to-start activity relationships that have discretionary dependencies. In other words, we have the ability to move them forward if we'd like. An example of this is that we might be able to begin user testing of a new mobile app three months before the schedule completion of the app beta by instead releasing an alpha version that might have a more limited feature set and a larger number of bugs and unfinished areas of work, but would still allow us to begin to get some feedback that we could use to shape our final product moving forward.

Lagging activities, on the other hand, are possible regardless of the type of activity relationship that might exist or the kind of dependency that might be at play. An example of lagging activity is that we must wait three days after pouring a foundation before we proceed with our construction work on a new building. Of course, we could wait four, five, six, or more days as well, we just have to wait at least those three days prior to beginning any of our additional work. To visualise this in a manner similar to how we might show it in a precedence network diagram, let's look at this example. Again, we might decide that production of an app beta must be completed before we can start prerelease user testing, but it might be possible to move this forward, in which case we might write this relationship instead as something similar to FS -3 months.

In other words, we need to finish the application beta before we can start prerelease user testing, but we're actually moving that forward three months on the schedule of the project, so we're going to begin that user testing three months prior to the completion of the preceding activity. Here, we may prefer to begin testing later, but we could begin it at this alpha stage. Leads are often leveraged when we're using schedule compression techniques, when we're trying to fast track a lot of our work in order to catch up on our schedule or to move forward in a more expedited manner. An example of a lag at play might be that we have to begin installing our kitchen furnishings before we can begin testing that cooking equipment.

In other words, the equipment needs to be installed before we can begin testing it, but we don't necessarily need to have all of the equipment installed before we begin any of that testing. We could say, though, that it's going to take at least three days before we've installed enough of our kitchen furnishings to begin the testing process. In this case, we would write this sort of relationship as SS +3 days. In other words, we can start testing our equipment before we've finished installing it, but we have to wait at least three days before that process can begin. Lags are often a source of schedule bottlenecks when improperly managed, but these can be mitigated to an extent using schedule compression techniques that we'll discuss later on.

Oftentimes, we express leads as negative numbers and lags as positive numbers in project management software. Consider this as a way of talking about the relationship in time between two different elements. If it's start-to-start +3 days, then we can begin working on the next task 3 days after we've begun the preceding activity. If, on the other hand, we say that there is a finish-to-start relationship -3 months, that means that 3 months before finishing the activity, we can begin working on its successor as well. This provides us some more granularity than the pure sort of activity relationships of finish to finish, finish to start, start to finish, or start to start can offer us and can help us to more effectively manage our project schedule and activity sequencing.

RESOURCE CALENDARS

Understanding the relationship between different activities and what dependencies might exist, as well as how we sequence them, is only half of the picture. Of course, in order for us to complete these activities, we have to move outside of the theoretical and into the actual, real world of our project team and the resource constraints that we might have.

Resource calendars are a great tool to use in order to better understand when our limited resources are available and how they can best be applied to our project work. Resource calendars identify working days and shifts when certain resources are either available or in use. These are useful in managing the utilisation of resources and in assigning resources to different project activities. Resource calendars enable more efficient use of resources as well because they help us to visualise when there might be downtime or gaps within our resource usage and how we can best utilise those resources at all times. Resource calendars may also include some other key attributes aside from just dates and whether that resource is at work or not on any particular activity.

These include geographic considerations, especially if we have to have that resource in a certain location for an activity to be completed, productivity information that lets us know how quickly similar resources might be able to work on the same task so that we can most efficiently allocate tasks to the right resources, as well as quality data that can let us know how well each different resource might perform, and what sort of rework or risk might be entailed with assigning any given activity to a certain resource. Let's take a look at an example of a simple resource calendar. Here, we know that we can begin our work on the 15th of the month and that we have 5 different activities that need to take place.

Activity 1 will require 20 units of activity. This could be hours, it could be days, it could be whatever sort of generalised unit that we're using in order to speak about these different activities using the same language. Activity 2 requires 3 units of work, activity 3 18 units, 4 15 units, and activity 5 4 units. We also have 3 different types of resource groups available to us. Our red team is able to complete up to 5 units of work per day. Our blue team can accomplish up to 10 units of work per day while our green team can accomplish just 1 unit of work per day. How can we best put all of these different resources to work in order to complete these activities as expeditiously as possible?

One answer might look something like this. We see that activity 2 is being completed by the green team over the Book of 3 days since they can complete 1 unit of work per day. Our blue team, which might be our strongest, fastest working and include the most people, is able to accomplish activities 1 and 3 over a Book of 4 days. That's because they're able to complete the first 20 units of work associated with activity 1 within the first 2 days, and then on the 17th and 18th of the month, they're able to accomplish the remaining 18 units of work, which is less than the 20 that they'd theoretically be capable of. At the same time, we might apply our red team, which can complete 5 units of work per day, toward activity 4, which consists of 15 total units of work.

After that, we would assign them on the fourth day of the project to activity 5 because they're able to certainly complete those 4 units of work, seeing as their normal capacity would be up to 5 different units. Of course, we might decide to also use different resources due to constraints related to cost, availability, or scheduling. It could be that our blue team is super expensive to utilise, and our project schedule has more than enough time for the red team to do all of this work. If that were the case, we would, instead, decide to spread out this work over a longer period of time.

Regardless of how we weigh these different factors, the visualisation that a resource calendar allows can help with both planning and selection of resources so that we make sure that we have all of the members of our project team working as efficiently as possible toward accomplishing our project's goals.

BOTTOM-UP ESTIMATING

Of course, determining logical relationships between activities is one thing, but when we want to move forward in sequencing those activities that don't necessarily have to be completed in any particular order or when we're making sequencing decisions where we've got more discretion, we're going to have to turn, not only to our resource availability, but also to developing a better understanding of how long each activity might take to accomplish.

Bottom-up estimating is a method for estimating project duration or cost. It combines estimates for activities or work packages in order to estimate a larger portion of the project. We can decompose these activities as far as appropriate to assist in estimating, but we can't simply add our way to full project estimates due to differences in resources, activity concurrence, and activity dependencies. It could be that we can work on several activities at the same time, and it could be that some activities can only be started after others are underway or have been completed in full. Furthermore, we might assign different types of resources to different activities, much as we just saw in our example with the resource calendar.

Let's take a look at an example of a variety of activities for our project. Here we see different activity identification numbers, a number of days that are expected for similar resources to accomplish each of these activities, and then a list of dependencies. For example, activities 2 and 3 can only be started after activity 1 has been completed. Activity 4 can only take place after activity 3, and so on. The assumptions here are that we have unlimited and identical resources and that our total work is going to take 26 resource days to be completed. Our minimum actual duration here would be 20 days of time. This is based on the various dependencies that we can see.

It takes 5 days to complete activity 1 at which point we can begin activities 2 and 3. However, activity 4 can't begin until activity 3 is completed. At this point, we would need to add 5 and 6, the length of activities 1 and 3, getting 11 to date. At that point, we can begin work on activity 4, which will serve as the predecessor to activities 5 and 6. Adding the 4-day duration of activity 4 to the 11 days that have passed so far, we find ourselves at a duration of 15 days. From here, we can move forward on activities 5 and 6.

Because these can take place concurrently, we can take the 15 days that have transpired thus far and add an additional 3 days to this from activity 6, marking 18 total days of project work so far. Our final activity, activity 8, can only be completed after activity 6 is completed. Adding another 2 days onto the end of our 18, we arrive at this minimum duration of 20 actual days.

Of course, in order to begin building a broad estimate of our project's total duration, we also have to arrive at our estimate for the duration of each of these individual activities. Let's take a look at some of the estimation techniques that can assist in this regard.

ESTIMATION TECHNIQUES FOR SCHEDULING

I t's impossible to discuss how we can develop our schedules and estimates for activity durations without also talking about the type of resources that we can apply toward our project's work. Various activity resource estimates determine the amount of work effort that's going to be required for tasks to be completed.

We can also determine which resources could be used in order to complete each of these different activities. Activity duration estimates, on the other hand, determine how long completion options may take for each of the different resource options that we could choose to utilise. When we merge these two areas of estimating duration and estimating the resources required to complete project work, we're able to determine which resources should be utilised for each of these activities, as well as determine the resources and work effort that will be required based on the decisions that we make.

We should try to use similar assumptions about resources about duration whenever possible, and we're going to have to progressively elaborate and refine these estimates as time progresses. Oftentimes, we may have a rough idea of duration and who we might assign to a particular activity early on, but if that resource is instead still working on another activity that's taking longer than expected, for example, we may find that we have to reassign work to another team later on in order to have it completed.

In order to estimate how many resources need to be applied to any particular activity or to estimate how long we expect that activity to take to complete, we can use one of three key estimating tools. The first of these is analogous estimating. In this case, we utilise historical data from similar activities or projects in order to estimate duration or cost information. Analogous estimating relies on parameters, like duration, budget, size, weight, complexity, and more in order to directly compare two items, one we're working on now with one that we have all of the facts about necessary.

A simple example of this might be if we work in a factory where we regularly produce some sort of machinery or widget that's very similar to the ones that came before it. If we know that 2 complete widget number 12, 424 took $10, 000 in 3 months, then it's likely that we could estimate widget 12, 425 identical in almost every respect to take about the same amount of cost and time in order to be completed. Analogous estimating techniques are useful when project specifics aren't necessarily well known or if they are extremely similar to ones that have come before.

Analogous estimating is less costly and time consuming than other estimation methods because we're essentially doing a simple comparison between something we know a lot about and something that we don't have all the information about just yet. However, it's also less accurate than other methods for this reason. Analogous estimating is most useful when there is expected to be substantial similarity between the two compared factors. Our widget example is a prime case where we might use analogous estimating because what we are expecting to build is so similar to what we've done in the past. It's also possible sometimes to cobble together different factors from other historical projects in the past and use several of these factors to create a composite analogous estimate of what might be expected from this project.

For example, if we know that we're going to be building a house and that the kitchen will be very similar to one house we've built before, while the rest of the house will be very similar to another that we've built in the past, we might be able to combine analogous estimates for these different components into one whole estimate of what it might take in order to build out this new house. Parametric estimating is the second method that we should discuss. This involves developing a formula that we can use in order to create our project duration or cost estimates. Project parameters and historical data are jointly leveraged here in order to generate these estimates.

We're using information about this project, as well as historical data related to time or cost in particular in order to create this formula that can give us our estimates of duration or cost. As you would expect, the quality of the data and the sophistication of the model we use are key accuracy factors here. For example, let's say that we are in the road construction business, that we are building out a new highway, we know that 1 mile of road costs $1 million to create over the span of 2 months.

If we are now bidding for a new project, which is going to encompass 3 miles of road, we might know that this is going to 3 times the work, and as such, we could create a very simple formula that would let us know that 3 miles of road might be estimated to cost 3 times as much and last 3 times as long. Some of the key assumptions that we've made in using this simple model are that there's going to be a similar deadline so that we are working on this at a similar pace to our prior project, that there's similar geography that we're dealing with here so that we're not having to work on an area that's more complex, maybe requiring a bridge or our ability to overgo or to level out terrain that might have been more challenging than what we've seen in the past. We're assuming we're going to use similar road material and that we're going to have similar road specifications, the same number of lanes, for example, as we've seen in the past.

Furthermore, we're assuming that there will be a similar labour effort and cost involved, as well as similar strength and quality parameters for how much weight the road should be able to carry and how long it should be expected to last. Models can also be developed for parametric estimating that account for differences in these kinds of factors, so we don't necessarily have to assume so many key points as being the same. If, for example, we've done a two-lane road before and now we're going to do a four-lane one, we can create some sort of multiplier into our formula that would take this into account.

The same would be true if we were using concrete instead of asphalt, for example, if we knew enough about the cost of these different materials and how they might also impact our labour and construction process. Parametric estimating is also useful in creating three-point estimates, which are the last type of estimating that we need to discuss. Three-point estimating inherently accounts for a range of different possibilities, including the most optimistic outcome, the most likely outcome and the most pessimistic outcome that we feel is reasonable. There are two different methods that are commonly used for three-point estimating. These are the triangular and PERT methods.

The triangular distribution method weights optimistic, pessimistic, and most likely scenarios equally. In other words, we simply add together the most optimistic, the most pessimistic, and the most likely estimates, and then divide them by 3. In this formula, we're using our expected time equaling our optimistic estimate of time, our most likely, and our most pessimistic estimates. A similar formula could be used for cost as well, as we'll see later. An example of this method at work could involve hearing the following from one of our subject matter experts.

Optimistically, we think we can complete the project within 20 days. Worst case would be 75 days. I'd guess 35 days is most likely, though. In this case, we can plug in these 3 data points to our formula and arrive at an estimate of 43 and 1/3 days as our time expected based on our most likely, our pessimistic, and our optimistic estimates. However, oftentimes, our most likely estimate was developed for a reason. It's not simply something found in the middle of the most optimistic or pessimistic, but rather, those other two are outliers while our most likely estimate should be given a greater weight.

This is where the program evaluation and review technique or PERT method comes into play. This weighs the most likely scenario much more heavily than less likely ones. Here, we would still add together the optimistic and pessimistic outcomes along with the most likely outcome, but instead, we would multiply the most likely outcome by 4, and then divide the sum total here by 6 in order to provide a much greater weight to our most likely outcome. Here, if we use the same parameters we saw previously, an optimistic outcome of 20 days, a pessimistic outcome of 75, and a most likely estimate of 35, we would instead see that our expected time would end up being 39 and 1/6 days as opposed to 43 and 1/3. Let's take a look at another example that compares these two methods.

We might hear from another one of our team members that if the permit comes through, we can be finished in three months, though four is more likely. If not, we can be delayed 12 months reapplying for the permit. If we use the triangular method here, we would have an optimistic outcome of 3 months, a most likely of 4, and a full 16 months, including the 4 we would consider most likely, if our permit were to be delayed.

Here, we would see an estimated time of 7 2/3 months from the triangular method. Applying the exact same variables into the PERT method though, we would instead arrive at an expected time of 5 5/6 months. This should be our more likely estimate given that it's relatively unlikely that our permit would need to be delayed. As such, we would probably consider the PERT method to be the more responsible estimate of how long this project can take.

CONTINGENCY AND MANAGEMENT RESERVES

No matter how well we estimate our project duration for each of our activities, something will always pop up. Someone might call in sick, there might be work that takes longer than expected, we might decide that additional features need to be added or that they weren't fully defined in the first place. In any of these cases, having some reserve in our schedule is the only way that we can account for these kinds of issues.

Contingency reserves provide a buffer to protect against uncertainty in a project. These are useful for both schedules and for budgets, and they're designed in a very similar fashion for each of these. Contingency reserves help to offset the potential impact of identified risks. These are areas where we know something might go wrong, and so we've provided ourselves with some cushion to help mitigate this effect. Understanding of risks and of potential impacts is necessary in order to determine what level of reserve might be appropriate for our project's needs. Contingency reserves can be planned at either the activity level or grouped into larger buckets of tasks.

Thinking back to the example of creating Twitter integration for our photo-sharing application, there are a variety of different activities that need to be accomplished there. It could be that we build in contingencies for each of those activities or at that higher work package level. These reserves may be expanded, contracted, or removed as project work progresses. If we've completed the task without having to use any or all of our contingency time, we can go ahead and remove that accordingly. If we determine that additional risks might be encountered along the way that would call for larger reserves, we can make that change as well.

Just the same, we can lower the amount of reserves if we determine that we've been too cautious in our initial planning. Reserves should be clearly separated from the actual estimates and schedules that we produce so that we have a reasonable understanding of what our actual estimated duration might be and what area in the schedule is specifically there to provide us with a bit more time, if necessary. Management reserves are the other kind of reserves that we might use within our project.

These reserves offset the potential impact of unidentified risks, in other words, the unknown unknowns, the things that we don't know could potentially arise and impact the project. These, again, may be applied to either schedules or to project budgets, and they allow for completion of unforeseen work that remains within the project scope. If we determine that completing a new task is going to be required in order to meet our existing objectives, that's the sort of activity that management reserves would call for.

Management reserves are not for use on out-of-scope work, nor should they be included in our schedule baseline. They should, however, be included in project duration requirements so that when we speak to the client, to our customer, or to the project sponsor, we provide them with the best estimate of how long we think the project might take. Remember, under promising and over delivering is always key, and so providing some room for these management reserves can ensure that, in the worst case, we're actually on time, rather than running behind from the customer's perspective. Even so, the baselines that we use to control our schedule may need to be modified if management reserves are used.

If, for example, something comes up early in the project that is going to take another week in order to accomplish, we might draw on our management reserves in order to accommodate this issue. However, it would be unfair to ourselves and provide a poor idea of our actual performance to then consider ourselves to be a week behind for the rest of the project. Instead, that baseline should be shifted in order to accommodate the fact that our management reserves were utilised so that we retain the best idea of how we are performing.

THE CRITICAL
PATH METHOD

E arlier, we talked about sequencing activities, understanding the dependencies that one another might have on each other, and figuring out how the duration of each of those might have some interplay with how long it takes our project to be completed. When we looked at that example of how different activity prerequisites might add up toward our total project duration, we were actually beginning to calculate what's known as the critical path.

Using a critical path method, especially with a precedence diagram the way that we've done before, visualises our project work and identifies the most critical project activities. It shows when actions may be required if project activities fall behind schedule by highlighting which activities are most important to the project being completed on time. The longest direct line of duration that can be plotted between a project's activities from the project's beginning to end is what we call the critical path. This is also the shortest total line that can possibly be necessary for the project's works to be completed. It might seem like these two facts are a bit at odds with one another, so let's take a look at an example.

In this simple one, we have three different activities that take place simultaneously that we have to complete before a project can be considered finished. We would have an activity that takes six months, one that takes three, and another that takes two in order to accomplish. Here, our critical path would be activity 1 because it is the 1 that's going to take the longest to complete. We can't finish the project until all 3 of these are done, and activity 1 will take the longest. Any of the activities we find along the critical path are, as you might expect, known as critical path activities. Any delay within these critical path activities will likely result in a delay to the whole project. Activities not on the critical path, on the other hand, are more flexible in nature.

Consider activity 2, because it's only going to take 3 months to complete and because we can work on it simultaneously while activity 1 is underway, it could be that we begin them at the same time, or we might determine that we want to start activity 2 later on. These activities not on the critical path offer greater flexibility. Let's take a look at a more realistic example with multiple activities taking place at the same time. Here, we see that we move from A1 into B1 and A2 at the same time, and then once B1 is completed, we can work on both A3 and B2. Once B2 is completed, we can work on C1 and B3, and once B3 and A4 are both completed, we can wrap up the project with activity 5.

How will we go about identifying the critical path for this sequence of activities? Well, Of course, it would start with the very first activity on the project. Once A1 is completed though, we can move on to either A2 or B1. Assuming that both of these take place at the same time, B1 would be the activity on the critical path due to its longer duration. From there, we can move on to B2 and A3. Once again, B2 would be the critical path activity because it will take longer to complete. From here, both C1 and B3 are possible, and you guessed it, C1 would be our critical path activity here due to its longer duration. From there, we can move on to B3 or A5 based on C1 being completed, but notice that B3 is also one of the predecessor activities for A5.

In other words, both C1 and B3 have to be completed before we can move on to A5. Once A5 has been completed, we can find ourselves at the end of the project. In any case, such as with A2, A3, and A4 where we have some additional time in which those activities can be completed, this time is known as either float or slack. We only find a float or slack on activities that are off of the critical path. And while typically this time provides us some flexibility with which we can optimise what resources we apply to any activity, we can also apply some schedule compression techniques, when necessary, in order to ensure that these items remain off the critical path and don't instead threaten to delay our project at large.

VISUALIZING PROJECT SCHEDULES

Project schedules are complex with a variety of activities taking place at any given time, relationships between these activities, different durations coming into play, and so on. As such, it's vital to have great ways to visualise our project schedules. There are many popular methods for visualising these schedules, and software packages can often present the same project data in a variety of different ways. These different visualisation styles can offer unique value, allowing us to look at our project in different ways, seeing how resources can better be utilised, and finding ways to reallocate our work and reorder our tasks in order to complete our work more effectively.

Activity-on-node charts are one example that we've already seen. In an activity-on-node chart, we have all of our activity information housed in each of these different rectangles, which are then connected using lines to show which different sort of relationships might exist between activities. We can either include duration information on the nodes themselves or on the lines in order to indicate what sort of relationship might exist between different activities. A milestone chart is another type of visualisation technique that we can use. These catalogue important dates and accomplishments in the project schedule and track both scheduled and actual start and completion dates wherever applicable.

A milestone chart might look something like this. Here, we might have several different columns indicating what the milestone is, the scheduled and actual start dates, as well as scheduled and actual completion dates. For our project charter sign- off, we might have a date of February 8, serving as both our scheduled and activity date of both start and completion given that this is a one-time event. We might, from there, say that we would like to commence production, and, in fact, find that we're running two days behind schedule at the beginning. Again, this is a single point in time so our completion and our start date would be the same.

However, for development of our first deliverable on the project, we might have a start date of April 1, again, going along with when production is first commenced and a scheduled completion date of July 1. It could be that we've completed this more quickly than originally expected despite starting a couple days behind and have an actual completion date of June 25. For development of deliverable 2, we might expect to begin our work on May 1 and actually do so, however, find that we're running slightly behind, finishing instead on July 5 instead of July 1. For our deliverables testing, this can begin as soon as we have some deliverables available, and so rather than on July 1, we were actually able to begin this on June 25, given that's when deliverable 1 was completed.

In addition, despite running a bit late on deliverable 2's completion, because we were running ahead of schedule on deliverable 1, we might finish a couple days before our initial target of August 1 for our deliverable testing to be completed. Gantt charts are another tool that can be very useful in visualising project work, in this case on a linear time scale that can help us to see exactly when different activities will take place. This is a great tool for quickly determining how processes relate to one another across time, and it can be useful in allocating resources and determining potential challenges and constraints as well.

This is particularly the case in more complex Gantt charts, which might use multiple different colours to represent different resources that could be working on our project at the same time. A relatively simple example of a Gantt chart in play would include this one, showing an overlap between activities 1 and 2, and activity 3 taking place entirely within the bounds of while activity 2's work is underway. Activity 4 might begin after activity 3 is complete, while activity 2 is still underway, and activity 5 might follow on shortly thereafter, eventually resulting in the culmination of our project's work.

By using these sorts of different visualisation tools, we can look at our project activities and better allocate resources and understand how to best control our project's progress.

SCHEDULE COMPRESSION TECHNIQUES

I n the last Book, we spoke a bit about resource levelling and resource smoothing and how they can be used to help optimise your utilisation of resources in the project environment. There are two other schedule compression techniques that you should also have in your tool belt along with these resource optimization techniques in order to help smooth out any issues you might have with your project schedule.

The first of these compression techniques is known as crashing. Crashing shortens completion time of activities by adding resources. This can be done in a variety of ways. You can bring in people to temporarily help out on the project, or you can have overtime occur where our existing resources work for longer in order to complete an activity more quickly in real time that might have happened if they were working only at the normal schedule. Crashing should only be utilised when necessary and as affordably as possible. It's very easy for budgets to get out of control when we start talking about running processes longer than expected.

It could be that we have to use equipment that we don't own, that we have instead rented or leased from another provider, and if we overuse it, if we consume more than we had initially expected, this can drive our costs up significantly. That's not to include the additional costs of labour that are associated with causing our team to work longer as well. Crashing should only be used for critical path activities because using overtime on non-critical path activities doesn't make any sense. By their very definition, we have longer to complete those, and therefore, we should instead focus on, perhaps, using our resources more quickly or figuring out how to better optimise their allocation, rather than having to apply crashing techniques to them directly.

However, keep in mind that delays to non-critical path activities may, in fact, end up placing them on to the critical path. We had originally thought that we had longer to complete these, but due to how long they've taken, they're now holding up the rest of the project and would then become eligible candidates for crashing to occur. Again, types of crashing that exist include overtime, as well as adding any additional resources, but we could also pay for expedited delivery if we're waiting on some sort of asset to arrive from a procurement source.

It could be that our work cannot begin until we've received a shipment of new tools or material, and so by receiving that more quickly, we're able to bump up our project schedule and help ensure that we remain on track. Crashing results in higher costs in almost every case, but also results in higher risk and potentially lowers quality. After all, we're simply working our team too hard, or we might be pushing our machinery or our fabrication tools to the limits by using them for longer than they were initially intended or designed for. Activities that are reliant on truly limited resources cannot be crashed effectively because there's simply a limit to how much time those resources can be applied.

If, for example, we have a few key team members who are absolutely essential to an activity taking place, we can only add so much overtime to their plate before they simply have to go to sleep. So in these sorts of cases, we have limits on the amount of work that we can do in order to accelerate our schedule. This is another reason why creating proper estimates, as well as effective contingency and management reserves from the beginning is so important. It helps to keep us from running into situations where we are unable to move forward our schedule in order to meet up with our estimates. Second, there is also fast-tracking. Fast-tracking reschedules sequential tasks in order to overlap in part or entirely. However, this can only be utilised when activities can overlap, in other words, when they have a discretionary dependency between each other.

In the case of mandatory dependencies where one absolutely must be finished before the next can begin, we can't fast-track these activities. Fast-tracking may be utilised for activities that are off the critical path for reasonable purposes. Oftentimes, we want to limit the use of any schedule compression to the critical path, but we might determine that, for example, it would be very low risk to fast-track an activity that precedes a much higher risk activity. By doing so, we might end up providing ourselves with more contingency time for that higher-risk activity by completing the low- risk one earlier on.

As with crashing, fast-tracking has the potential to add risk to our project to lower its quality or even result in some rework being necessary because we've jumped ahead in our project schedule. And if something has changed with a preceding activity along the way, we might have to go back and make further revisions to the activity we have fast-tracked accordingly. As such, both of these schedule compression techniques should be used as sparingly as possible, and the more time you spend in making sure that your estimates are effective and your reserves are robust, the less you'll find yourself having to deploy either of these techniques.

KEY CONCEPTS

We covered an immense amount of material in this chapter, but the key concepts are still quite clear. Before we schedule our projects, it's important to make some key determinations. What methodology will we use? What level of accuracy is important? What units of measure will we employ? What rules should be laid out for performance measurement and control? What reporting format should we use and how often? With a framework for scheduling in place, we can now move forward to define the activities we must undertake in order to meet project objectives.

We can determine what order for these activities makes the most sense and how each of these activities relate to one another. Must we wait until one activity is totally completed before beginning another? Or is it possible to begin work sometime earlier? Would we simply prefer that that kind of order be followed, or is it absolutely necessary? How much wiggle room do we have, and how can we use it to best meet our project's goals? What tools and estimating techniques can we use to better understand our project work, better plan when activities are addressed, and better gauge the resources and time necessary to complete each task?

By answering these kinds of questions, we can discover our project's critical path, that is, the line of activities that represents the minimum duration of our project. By closely managing the critical path, we can help ensure that our project remains on schedule. Techniques like crashing, in other words, adding more resources or overtime, and fast-tracking, where we begin activities earlier than initially planned can help us meet any challenges that become apparent when managing the critical path and help ensure that we remain on Book.

While outlining a project's full schedule in great detail up front might seem ideal, that is, Of course, not always possible. Indeed, in today's agile project environments, we don't necessarily even want a grand blueprint right from the start because we want or need to reserve the ability to make changes along the way. In the next chapter, we'll look at how Agile environments are structured and how you can adapt the scheduling techniques you've learned here to any project methodology.

IMPLEMENTING
AGILE METHODS

I n this chapter, we'll begin by looking at the differences between project life cycles in order to better understand how Agile project environments differ from predictive, plan-driven ones, and to see how these philosophies intermingle in iterative project environments. Then, we'll move on to look at some of the roles unique to Agile environments, learning how scrub masters differ from product owners and how responsibilities are divided in managing projects.

After that, we'll take a look at how to plan effective sprints, a defined period of time in which a component of the project work is completed and how tools like scrum boards and burndown charts can help in meeting our goals. Finally, we'll look at two types of meetings unique to Agile environments, daily standups and scrum retrospectives and learn how each of these are essential to an Agile project's success. Let's get started.

TYPES OF PROJECT LIFE CYCLES

Projects can be managed in many different ways depending on what is common for your organisation, what your particular project calls for, and what your preferences might be as a project manager. In general, there are a few different philosophies for how project life cycles can be managed that can be seen to be on a spectrum of sorts. This begins with a plan-driven model.

Closer to the centre, we see a more iterative or incremental model, and then on the other side, we have Agile project life cycles. When it comes to plan-driven project life cycles, all of our requirements should be defined before work moves forward. All of our work is delivered together at the end of the project. Changes to our project plans are discouraged, and change control is a very rigid process, something that we want to use as little as possible because, hopefully, our plans are really solid and well detailed for the work that is to come, and key stakeholders are mostly involved upfront and at key milestones along the way, instead of on a daily basis.

Instead, they're brought in at those key points to ensure that the project is moving forward successfully and is still on track, but otherwise, the work is largely left to the project team to continue unencumbered. A more iterative or incremental approach could be considered a hybrid of the plan-drive and agile life cycles. In this case, requirements are defined and revised at regular intervals, so rather than defining all of our requirements at the outset, instead we take whatever is most likely to come next, and we think about those in greater detail, perhaps having broad plans for what will come later at the same time.

Project results can also be delivered incrementally in an iterative lifecycle. Here, we may have multiple components to our end product that we need to ship eventually, but there's some value to be had from delivering certain components earlier on. Changes should be discussed and implemented at regular intervals, unlike with a plan-drive model where we try to discourage changes and hold ourselves to an extremely rigid change control process. And key stakeholders are involved more regularly, but again, at intervals rather than on an ongoing basis. In the case of Agile project life cycles, requirements are frequently and continuously defined.

This is a continuously ongoing process, rather than something that we put all of our energy and time into up front. Rather, we continue to define our activities and our requirements along the way as we learn more from our work and see which portion of our objectives could best be accomplished next. As part of this, results are delivered as they are finished, so we receive these on a regular basis, as soon as these new changes are put into place. When you think about software development projects that have nightly builds, this is an example of an ideal Agile environment where we are constantly shipping our latest version, even if the changes are very, very small.

Furthermore, any of these change requests are incorporated in real time. This doesn't mean that they aren't documented and that we don't have an approval process in place, but rather, we are continuously in this process of figuring out what changes need to be made in order to better meet our objectives, rather than trying to hold onto these changes for some sort of formal, regular change control process that might only occur, for example, every few weeks. Key stakeholders are also involved continuously in an Agile project environment, either themselves or through their representative, the product owner.

Adaptive management is often chosen when projects must remain flexible or must remain open to change based on project progress. Activities from all of the different process groups regularly intermingle within these adaptive environments unlike in a plan- driven model where we might have some overlap, but we would generally expect to go from initiating to planning to executing while monitoring and controlling all the way until we're ready to close out our project's work.

In the case of an adaptive environment, one that's more agile in nature, we would expect to revisit our project charter on a regular basis. Furthermore, continuous feedback from key stakeholders is essential to ensuring that our work and objectives remain aligned with one another along the way. This is especially the case because we may continue updating our charter to make sure that it aligns best with our business case as we move forward, rather than in a more plan-driven model where the charter acts as a solid document that really shouldn't be touched or modified at all after it's received its approval.

When it comes to planning, plans must consistently be adapted to our shifting objectives along the way. It's best, as such, to plan the high level early on and add details shortly before work is undertaken, rather than spending a lot of time up front putting into place the details of work that's far into the future and that's liable to change substantially before we would actually begin to address it. When it comes to executing, work is completed in iterations rather than in one long series. Rather than the project simply having a beginning and an end, we have a variety of what are known as sprints, where after a certain period of time, we have a reset where we are able to see how much we've accomplished and set our objectives for the next sprint.

As such, we move forward incrementally, always delivering some sort of progress at the end of each of these sprints while we move toward completing all of our project objectives. This sort of system allows regular opportunities for review to occur and for us to tweak both how we're working and what we're working on to ensure that it continually aligns with our shifting objectives.

It's important to track our progress against both short and long-term targets within adaptive environments. We want to make sure that we're not just completing the work that's involved in the sprint to come, but rather that we're also moving toward our broader objectives over time. When it comes to monitoring and controlling, an adaptive environment's backlogs are key to managing performance within these environments. These backlogs are a list of the features or activities that still need to be developed or completed before we could consider our project work concluded. The backlog should have a list of all of the remaining activities necessary to complete the project, and over time, we take activities from this backlog and move it into our active work environment.

Once the backlog has been depleted, we could consider the project to be complete. The iterative nature of adaptive environments provides a wealth of opportunities to measure our progress along the way, and changes can be requested and implemented more quickly than we would see in predictive environments. As such, there is a much more dynamic relationship between what we are able to measure and how we're able to immediately react to that measurement to ensure that we're constantly moving toward a more efficient process and accomplishing our goals. Finally, when it comes to closing out projects, the iterative nature of adaptive environments means that less value is lost if work is closed off prematurely.

In a purely plan-drive system, it could be that right up until very close to the end of the project, there's not much value that's actually been created. Rather, there are many different subcomponents that are 80 or 90% of the way toward having value toward our end user, but until we are able to cobble these together and truly complete all of the work on them, we haven't actually created anything of use. In an adaptive environment, we can typically use what we've created along the way because the focus is on creating something usable, some tangible measure of progress that we can close off by the end of each of these different sprints. The residual value is more likely to exist thanks to how this work is structured as opposed to in a more plan-driven environment.

KEY ROLES IN AGILE PROJECT ENVIRONMENTS

As compared to more plan-driven, predictive project management approaches, Agile project teams tend to have a different set of key roles. A greater emphasis is placed on stakeholder involvement and on team empowerment within these Agile environments. Rather than the project manager more directly delegating tasks to every team member, a greater focus is placed on facilitating group team effort instead. This begins with the scrum master.

The scrum master is responsible for coordinating team work on sprints and ensures that team members are unimpeded by distractions along the way. The scrum master is here to facilitate progress, not to directly manage team members' work. Rather, their focus is on empowering team members to do the work they need to do on their own to help meet project objectives. The project owner is one of the other key roles within an Agile project environment. The product owner serves as the representative for project stakeholders, whether it be the customer, the user, the project sponsor, or whomever the end recipient of the project's work might be. For this reason, the project owner is often also referred to as the voice of the customer.

The project owner must communicate with stakeholders about project work because they serve as the conduit between however many stakeholders there may be within the project and with the project team responsible for implementing the project's work. The product owner has the ultimate authority on the project's scope, authority, and funding and manages the backlog for the project in coordination with the scrum master. Stakeholders are, Of course, key to any project environment, and that's no different within an Agile environment than it would be in any other. Stakeholders are anyone who may impact or be impacted by a project's work or its result. These stakeholders are represented by the product owner who serves as their primary liaison to the project team.

Of course, in addition to stakeholders and the scrum master and the product owner, we also have the team members themselves who are responsible for carrying out the project's work. Team members complete backlog items and typically sign up for tasks based on skill sets and activity priority. It's up to the team members themselves to determine which tasks they're going to take upon themselves next, while the scrum master and the project owner work together to determine which backlog items should have the highest priority and be presented to the team members as most immediately important to complete. Teams are autonomously managed, directed, and organised within Agile environments.

Rather than where you've got the project manager telling each member what they should be working on, this is a much more organic system, where team members are expected to take on the work that they reasonably can in the areas in which they can contribute and help toward the broader goal of the mission. They set their own estimates for work and self-assign enough tasks to fill each sprint's duration.

The scrum master can help in this regard, helping team members to understand what a proper balance of tasks might be and how they could be allocated among team members who might equally desire taking on the role, but it's up to the team members themselves to take responsibility for each of these different work packages or activities that need to be accomplished and ensure that it's completed within the sprint's timeline.

PLANNING SPRINTS

I n Agile environments, work takes place in iterations, or more commonly what's known as sprints. Each of these sprints should result in a deliverable or at least a clearly defined component of a deliverable being produced. Sprints should last a short, agreed-upon period of time. Often two weeks is used as a good barometer because it provides enough time for some substantial work to be completed by the project team without going so long as to not allow for the agile nature of this environment to have its benefits.

Sprint planning meetings are focused on choosing work items from the backlog. These backlogs, Of course, eventually include all of our project requirements. Of course, they might not at first because we might not be aware or have fully defined what all of our project requirements are at the outset. Rather, this information is something that we become more familiar with and that we can define in greater detail as project work gets underway. This, Of course, goes back to the core principle of progressive elaboration that is inherent within almost any project environment.

The product owner is responsible for maintaining and prioritising this backlog of items, although they can also coordinate with the scrum master in order to help make sure that the process they choose and the way that the backlog is organised aligns well with the team's capabilities. Requirements in the backlog may be either added, removed, or changed at the product owner's determination. It's really up to the product owner to determine what the project team should be working on within each of these sprints. The backlog that the product owner creates can be managed using software tools or simply sticky notes on a whiteboard, which remains a really common way for Agile teams to work together, especially if they can share a workspace and work together in close quarters.

Of course, there are software tools that will replicate much of this functionality, but allow teams that might be at many different geographic locations to work better together, as well as allow for greater detail than might be able to be found on any one sticky note and the ability to link to other organisational documents that might be relevant to each of those action items. Of course, these action items in the backlog can also be known as user stories. That's because they tend to be written in a narrative fashion that describes the desired results that should come from each task being completed. Rather than simply being a dry documented list of requirements, here the idea is more to define what the end result should be, rather than the specific process that should be taken to get there.

Of course, details about requirements or limitations can be included, but our chief goal here is for a result to come about, not for a particular process to have necessarily been followed. A scrum board often might look something like this with a variety of items sitting in our backlog waiting to be moved in on the next sprint. At the sprint planning meeting, we might go ahead and move several of these items over to the In Progress category. Other items might be in review after work on them has been, at least, provisionally completed, and, Of course, items that have passed review could be found within this Completed category as well. Of course, oftentimes there are many more than the small handful of notes that you see here on this scrum board.

We could have dozens or hundreds of items within a backlog, many more in progress at the same time, several more in the review, and the completed list should continue to grow as we move towards our project's completion. Of course, it's not enough to just have a list of what items have been completed in total for the project. Half of the reason why we are working in these smaller sprints is because it allows us to have a more concrete idea of what we're working on now and what has recently been completed. That's where burndown charts come in handy. Burndown charts visualise progress of work during a sprint versus our project plans.

One axis of these burndown charts represents the remaining time within a sprint, while the other axis represents the estimated duration of remaining work. Burndown charts can be a useful tool for providing near real-time feedback to teams regarding progress, and you'll often see them posted right on scrum boards so that teams can see on a daily basis how they're doing compared to what they've planned for that sprint. Here's an example of a simple burndown chart. On our Y axis, we have remaining projected days. In other words, if we know that we could complete a general amount of work within a single day, how many days' worth of work do we think we have left? On the X axis, we have the number of sprint days completed thus far.

In blue, you'll see that we have backlog items completed, while in orange, you'll have the number of backlog items planned. Of course, if we had 15 days' worth of work, by the end of 15 days, we would hope that we've completed all this work. As you can see, we actually do get there at the end, but any sort of project environment is bound to be more organic than a simple straight linear line can offer. Here, for a while, we were actually ahead of schedule. However, closer to the end of our sprint, we had more days' worth of work remaining than we actually had days to go. We were able to make up this lost time, however, and still end up finishing our spring and all of our objectives on time.

If this weren't the case, then we would see that our blue backlog line would still be somewhere higher up on the Y axis, leaving additional work to be discussed during the next scrum retrospective and potentially to be added to the next sprint.

SCRUM MEETINGS

T wo key types of meetings are unique to Agile environments when compared with traditional, predictive, plan-driven project teams. The first of these are daily standup meetings, which are an important component of the Agile environment. These daily standups should involve the full team and be held at the same place and time each day. They should be brief in nature, no more than 15 minutes if possible, with a very tight objective of three key points being shared by each team member.

The first of these is what did I accomplish yesterday? Second, what will I work on today? And the third, is anything preventing me from doing my work? This not only keeps colleagues abreast of what you're working on and serves an important role in accountability given that each team member has to tell the entire team what it is that they've accomplished and what they're going to be working on, but it also provides an opportunity for these challenges to be addressed by the scrum master who works to solve these issues that are preventing team members from accomplishing their work.

Product owners may attend, but should not actively participate in the scrum meeting, which is really for the benefit of the team itself and for them to understand how they're going to work on what's already been agreed upon. Any conversations about new requirements or any technical topics or questions should be held outside of the daily standup, perhaps even immediately before or after, but the daily standup itself should be kept for discussing only the work that's already under consideration. It's important for the scrum master to facilitate but not micromanage this discussion, rather try and allow the team all of the autonomy possible in accomplishing their mission and make sure that they have the tools and the ability to do so without getting in the way.

However, it is perfectly acceptable for the scrum master to ask insightful questions that can help to drive the conversation and help team members to decide how they should go about their work and how they should approach any challenges that might be inherent to it. Aside from these daily standup meetings, a different type of meeting occurs at the end of each sprint. These are known as scrum retrospectives. In this case, the scrum master, the product owner, and team members should all participate.

The goals of these scrum retrospectives are to understand what work was completed within the sprint that has just concluded, what work was planned for the sprint but remains incomplete, what work should be carried into the sprint, and how the project overall is progressing. Finally, this is also a valuable opportunity to address any lessons that have been learned and to document any key takeaways from this sprint that can help to guide our work moving forward.

This is also an opportunity to assess whether or not our requirements and our current backlog aligns to our shifting priorities for the project, or if work that we've learned from in this sprint might have caused us to consider changes to our work moving forward based on their representation of stakeholders and its invaluable opportunity for both the teams members accomplishing the project's work and the product owner responsible for the vision of the project's work to ensure that they remain consistently aligned before embarking on the next sprint.

PROJECT LIFE CYCLES

In this chapter, we learned how project life cycles differ from one another. We saw how scrum masters help facilitate project success and how product owners ensure the project teams are meeting stakeholders' needs. We learned how to plan effective sprints and how tools, like scrum boards filled with user stories describing action items we need to work on, as well as burndown charts describing how we're doing compared to our goals for a sprint, are central to Agile planning.

Finally, we saw how daily standups help the scrum master remove obstacles from the project team's way and ensure that team members are kept up to date on one another's status and how scrum retrospectives can help us understand what's been accomplished, what's to come, and what we've learned that can help us get there. While plan-drive and Agile life cycles can typically be thought of as two ends of a spectrum, it's important to remember just how much room lies in between the purest definition of each of these two forms.

Most projects fall somewhere in between these two extremes. We want to make plans, but also must remain adaptable to changing or developing requirements, stakeholder needs, market conditions, and more. We might develop a long-term plan, but handle the execution of activity batches using Agile-like methods. For the purposes of the CompTIA Project+ exam, only a high-level knowledge of Agile principles is necessary. However, there's much to be gained by mastering Agile principles. If you're interested in learning more, Amazon authors like Jeremy Jarrell, Stephen Haunts, Xavier Morera, and David Starr can help take you to the next step. Regardless of how agile or plan driven your project may be, understanding the core foundations of scheduling and budgeting can help guide you to success.

In the next chapter, we'll look more closely at the budgetary concepts and techniques that can help ensure your project's costs stay on track.

DEVELOPING PROJECT BUDGETS

I n this chapter, we'll begin by discussing the many factors that should be considered when estimating costs. Then, we'll look at how some of the estimation techniques we first applied to our project schedule can now be applied to our budget. After that, we'll discuss the importance of budgetary reserves and show how a baseline budget should be designed that properly captures both our cost estimates and the funds we've set aside for unexpected overruns.

Then, we'll move on to discuss the importance of expense tracking before introducing earned value management techniques that can help us quantitatively gauge how well we are performing on our project's work. Let's get started.

ESTIMATING COSTS

As is true with schedules, when it comes to estimating costs, there are a variety of factors that must be considered. Among these, Of course, are the cost of the activities themselves, but also financing considerations and funding prerequisites, such as milestones that might be attached to additional financing and funding that we need to move forward, as well as cash flow timing of when we have to make purchases and when we can expect to receive new money all come into play when developing our budget.

Furthermore, activity costs are rarely as simple as one headline number. Rather, these cost estimates themselves are made up of a variety of subcomponents, including labour costs, material costs, costs for equipment, facilities costs, and the costs of other services that might be required. Furthermore, it's not as simple as either paying our employees or buying everything we need. Rather, especially when it comes to large capital equipment and major expenses of that nature, oftentimes, we have to make additional decisions of whether to make or procure or if we're going to buy, lease, or rent any of the underlying equipment or tools that we may need in order to complete project work.

We can express costs in a variety of different fashions. It could be that we want to speak about each cost in the currency of its transaction. This might mean speaking about dollars in one area and euros in another if we're taking on a global project or if we have material expenses from a variety of different sources across the globe. We could also use a standardised currency at which point we'd need to have some sort of procedures in place for how we recognize exchange rates. We can also speak of costs in terms of staff hours or days if we're primarily concerned with the burden that's being placed on our human resources. When we estimate our costs, oftentimes, much as is true with the actual details of a requirement, we are going to learn more and be able to create greater detail over time. As such, early on in the project, our goal should be to create a rough order of magnitude for our expenses.

Oftentimes, it's generally accepted that such a rough order of magnitude can range from -25% to +75% of what we think the cost might actually be. Over time, we want to go ahead and fill in this estimate line with something more precise that can allow us to fund our project with a greater sense of accuracy. When we create these definitive estimates, our target should be within the -5 to +10% range, a much tighter range than where we had initially started. This still allows for a good amount of contingency in case unexpected expenses are incurred along the way, but should be definitive enough for us to move forward with our project's work with a good idea of what our budgetary requirements will be.

COST ESTIMATION
TECHNIQUES

T he techniques first introduced when we discussed estimating our project and activity durations can also be applied to our cost estimations as well. This begins with analogous estimating where we utilise historical data from similar activities or projects to guide us toward an idea of what the cost might be for a similar project or activity being undertaken now. Analogous estimating relies on parameters that allow activities to be compared with one another, and the strength of the comparison is key to the accuracy of this estimate.

If two things aren't very alike, it's going to be difficult to make an accurate assessment using analogous estimating as a tool. Our example from duration stands here as well. A widget that's very similar to one that was recently created and for which we might have a long history of creating similar projects might have cost $10, 000 before and taken 3 months to create. As such, we could expect this one to cost about the same and take about as long in order to create as well. Analogous estimating is useful when project specifics aren't well known because when they are well known, we can often use a more accurate and quantitative method, such as parametric estimating instead.

Analogous estimates are less costly and time consuming to

generate than other types of estimates, but they are less accurate as well by virtue of the fact that they aren't as quantitative. Analogous estimates are most useful when there is substantial similarity between the two compared factors. Of course, we can also create a composite analogous estimate using factors that are similar or traits that are similar for multiple projects and then bringing together the cost information for each of those different subcomponents and creating our estimate for this project overall. Parametric estimating is our second and often more precise estimating technique. Here, project parameters and historical data are jointly leveraged in order to generate our project cost estimates.

The quality of the data and the sophistication of the model that we create are the key accuracy factors here. Some of the different types of cost parameters that we might use in order to create a parametric formula might include the cost per square foot, cost per day, cost per mile, or cost per pound. Any of these different units allow us to discuss cost in a fashion that we can either estimate or measure directly. As we saw with scheduling, our example of creating one mile of road being extrapolated out to creating three miles of new road gives us an opportunity for simple parametric estimation. Three miles of road is three times the work, and we might expect that all else held equal, our estimated cost might be three times as much as creating one mile of road might be.

Of course, this doesn't take into account things like economies of scale that might actually be unlocked and result in a lower overall cost than we would expect based on simply multiplying out based on a distance metric alone. The more sophisticated of a model we can create, the better for our parametric estimates. We can, Of course, also feed this information into three-point estimates that we create, which inherently account for a range of different possibilities, among these being optimistic, most likely, and pessimistic outcomes. Both the triangular and the PERT methods are among the most commonly used here.

The triangular method weights the optimistic, pessimistic, and most likely scenarios equally, just as would happen when estimating activity durations. However, our formula naturally changes a bit. Now, we're talking about costs that are expected or estimated to occur. An example of this formula at work would be if one of our project team members came to us and said optimistically, we're looking at a project cost of about $50, 000. Worst case, I'd say $95, 000. I'd guess $65, 000 is most likely. If we plug these different variables into our cost formula here, we would see that we arrive at an expected cost of $70, 000 based on our optimistic, pessimistic, and most likely scenarios all being weighted equally.

In a PERT, or program evaluation and review technique method, we weigh the most likely scenario much more heavily than the less likely ones. In this case, that means taking the optimistic and pessimistic variables, adding them together with the most likely estimate multiplied by 4 and then dividing that sum total by 6. Revisiting the same example first introduced for triangular distribution, we would see that here we would now multiply the most likely answer of 65, 000 by 4.

By dividing this sum total by 6, we would arrive at a cost estimate of $67, 500, lower than the 70, 000 that we might have expected from the triangular distribution alone. In this case, we're weighting much more heavily toward our middle result, but that also will often provide us with a more accurate assessment, assuming that we put in the work necessary for our most likely estimate to be trustworthy.

BUDGETARY RESERVES

As is true with our schedule, it's important for us to set aside some reserves that can help us to deal with any budgetary issues that might arise. Both contingency and management reserves may be created and used for our budget. These contingency reserves help to offset the potential impact of identified risks, the ones that we know might have happened from the beginning of the project, or at least, the ones that we've caught along the way as we continue to define our activities.

These reserves are put into place to address those risks should they arise. Management reserves, on the other hand, help to offset the potential impact of unidentified risks, those that we can't foresee and that we did not expect to become an issue within the project. These reserves should only be used toward additional work or additional expenses that are still within the project scope, so this is not an opportunity for us at discretion to modify the goals or objectives of our project, but rather to make sure that we're able to overcome challenges that arise that would prevent us from accomplishing those goals.

The calculation methods that we might use in order to arrive at our contingency and management reserves include percentages of projected costs, the cost of a number of work periods if we're concerned about the amount of time that might be required to offset any challenges that arise, or we can define them in some sort of other quantitative nature, typically using a formula that can help to address what types of risks might emerge, how likely they would be, and what the overall impact of those risks could be to the project as well. One way we can go about calculating what our reserve amounts should be is use of the Monte Carlo method.

The Monte Carlo method uses thousands of simulations of project work to see when things might go wrong and when things might go right and what the different impacts of different activities within the project might be. If we are able to do our best work throughout the project, how much do we expect that might cost? If we have a relatively minor holdup occur on a relatively minor activity, what would the impact of that be? If we have a cascading series of failures across the critical path, what sort of contingencies might we need to have in place in order to assist with that as well? Contingency levels needed may be developed with a certain degree of confidence based on the results of these Monte Carlo simulations.

Contingency levels needed may be developed with a certain degree of confidence based on these results. By running the model and by having an idea of the probability of different risks emerging, we're able to create a model where we can say with a certain level of confidence what the standard deviation from the project's expected budget might be. As such, by having, for example, two standard deviations' worth of additional contingencies in place, we can with 95% certainty say that we'll have the budget necessary in order to complete all of our project's objectives, even if challenges arise.

DEVELOPING A BASELINE BUDGET

O ur baseline budget is what we'll be able to use in order to measure our project performance, how well we're doing, and if we're over or under budget. As such, it's important for us to get this baseline right. To do so, we should first make sure that ground rules for spending and budgeting are established.

This should include information on expenditure approval, budgetary authority levels for various team members, as well as any cost triggers or thresholds that might require additional approval, a meeting, or some sort of formal process to be followed before that expenditure can be undertaken. As part of developing a baseline budget, we should establish how expenses will be tracked and by whom. While the project manager will remain accountable for project expenditures regardless of how the budget is tracked, they're not always the one that will have the day-to-day purview over many expenditures that will occur.

Oftentimes, team members, or at least leaders of various parts of the team, will have the ability to undertake expenses on their own, at least to certain levels before additional approval might need to be sought. Ensuring that this kind of information is known by the team and well documented is just as important as the cost estimates themselves. Speaking of which, cost estimates may be attached to items within the work breakdown structure dictionary, allowing us to directly tie each of our activities and our work packages back to the cost estimates to complete them, as well as who's responsible for each of those activities being completed.

The baseline should include all of our estimated activity costs plus our contingency reserves based on those risks that we've identified while defining these requirements. However, management reserves should not be included within this cost baseline. Let's take a look at this in a visualisation. Here, we might start by having our activity cost estimates. In addition to these activity cost estimates, we should add our activity contingency reserve. From here, we might also have some additional contingency reserves added on top of our work package cost estimates. Here, we have two different levels of contingency reserves that may be tapped into, although it may be more appropriate for your environment to only include contingency reserves at either the activity or work package level. In any case, once all of our contingency reserves have been added to our activity and work package cost estimates, we've arrived at our cost baseline.

However, management reserves should still be added to this to help with any of the unidentified and unanticipated risks that might arise. Once we've added in our management reserves to our cost baseline, we arrive at our full project budget. Once we have a baseline and a budget in place, it's important for us to monitor over time how our project is performing compared to this baseline. Let's take a look at this example from the Project Management Body of Knowledge. Here, you can see that early on, our expenditures are tracking well below our cost baseline. Over time as project work progresses, additional funding is made available to the team based on each new period or milestone that's been reached. This pattern continues, but over time, you can see that our expenditures actually track above the cost baseline and begin to dip into our management reserves.

In this case, we actually finish both above the baseline and under the budget because these management reserves were in place to help deal with those unanticipated, unidentified risks that emerged at some point during this project's work. This is why having management reserves in place, along with the contingency reserves that are built into the baseline itself, is so important. It ensures that even when we are unable to foresee challenges that might arise, we'll have the resources necessary in order to surmount those successfully,

TRACKING EXPENSES

Once our budget is set and we have some documentation and procedures in place for how expenses should be handled, it's important that we use a unified, documented expense tracking process for all of our budget management. After all, if we don't keep good track of the money we're spending, how are we supposed to know how much we have left and how much we've spent so far. Oftentimes, we may manage expenses within our project management software directly, or we may use a dedicated accounting tool in order to fulfil this role.

It's important for us to capture as much information as possible about each of our expenses. This simply leads to better cost control and allows for easier generation of expense reports and visualisations that can help us understand our cost performance and share with key stakeholders who often are in charge of what funding our project team has available to us. Some of the key information that we should seek to capture includes account codes that can help us to directly tie activities and work packages to expenses, categories that can help us in our reporting to understand what types of expenses we are seeing and incurring in our project and what areas of the project are the ones incurring these expenses, key dates that give us information on when expenses might have first been agreed to and when they might be paid, especially in areas where we might owe the money later based on either a payment agreement having been made or perhaps a credit card purchase having been made on behalf of the team, information on the estimated and actual costs that have been incurred so that we can understand how well we have been doing in estimating our cost, and then the cost variance, or the difference between that actual and estimated cost.

Using these pieces of information, we can not only keep better track of our project's budget to date, but also hopefully convert this into useful lessons learned for our additional estimates moving forward on the project so that we can continue to be more accurate in the way that we project our expenses.

EARNED VALUE
MANAGEMENT

O ur last topic in this chapter is earned value management,
which can help us to better understand exactly how well
we are doing in our project environment, well and above
what we could expect to see based on only a dollar amount alone.
Here, we want to compare our project expenses to our value
creation thus far, not just any cost baseline or assumptions we
might have had based on the day and time that we find ourselves
in within the project.

Of course, if I told you that one project was over budget and the
other was under budget, you would be very likely to say that the
one that's under budget is the better project that's being better
managed right now. However, what if I went on to tell you that the
over budget project is actually ahead of schedule while the under
budget one is behind schedule. All of a sudden, it's a bit harder
to gauge which of these might be the more effective environment.
After all, we might be over budget right now because we're
actually doing our work more quickly than expected. In such a
case, we would consider the over budget project to actually be
the better one because we're over performing versus what we had
initially expected and therefore simply naturally incurring costs
more quickly.

We can make a few different calculations to help us understand our relationship between our budget and how much value has been created along the way. To do so, we need three key variables. The first of these is planned value, or PV. This is our budgeted cost for a work package or other specific work component. In other words, it's the estimate that we've made for what that work package should cost. There is the AC, which is our actual cost incurred for any of these work packages. This is based on the same standard used for our planned value estimates, so any expenses that we incur and that we consider part of the actual cost should be expenses that we had initially estimated as being part of that planned value. That way, we can be certain to compare apples to apples and not end up with an unfair comparison here where one cost has information that the other projected cost does not.

Third, there's earned value, or EV. This is the value of completed work to date as compared to the budgeted amount overall. Earned value is often calculated as a percentage of work completed. For example, if we said that 40% of work is completed and that we would expect a planned value of $10, 000 at completion, then to date, we would have earned $4, 000 in value based on our project work. Using these variables, we can calculate five different key metrics to help us understand how we're doing within our project. This includes cost and schedule variance, cost performance index, the schedule performance index, and our burn rate.

Our cost variance answers the question, is the project above or below budget? Here, our formula would be cost variance equal to earned value minus actual cost. If the result of this formula turns out to be negative, then we would consider our project to be over budget. If it's positive, we would be under budget. Let's look at an example. If we said that 50% of a $735, 000 project is complete, and so far the project team has spent $349, 000, we might then wonder, what is the present cost variance, and is the project team over or under budget? Well, 50% of $735, 000 is $367, 500. That would indicate that our earned value to date is $367, 500, or half of what we expect the project to be worth once it's complete.

Of course, our actual cost is given here as just $349, 000. So if we take that earned value and then we subtract from it the actual cost to date, we arrive at a cost variance of $18, 500, indicating that for now, at least, we're actually running under budget. Good work! Schedule variance comes next, and it's calculated in a similar fashion, answering the question, is the project ahead or behind schedule? Here, we would subtract planned value from our earned value. If we end up at a negative number, we would consider ourselves to be behind schedule, and if it's positive, then we would consider ourselves to be ahead of schedule. Let's look at an example here. Six months into a 12-month, $1. 2 million dollar project, $400, 000 of value has been created.

What is the present schedule variance, and is the project ahead or behind schedule? Well, we know that 6 months would equal half of our total schedule time based on a 12-month project window. As such, we should expect our planned value to be 50% of our budget, or the final value that we appraise our project as being worth. If that's the case, then our planned value would be $1. 2 million dollars times 0. 5, or half of the schedule. We should expect $600, 000 of work to be complete at this time based on this metric, but instead, we see that only $400, 000 of value have been created to date. As such, we would see a schedule variance of -$200, 000 here, indicating that this project is running behind schedule.

Let's look next at the cost performance index, which answers the question whether the project is on budget or not. We calculate this CPI index figure by dividing the earned value by our actual cost. Any result below 1. 0 would indicate a cost overrun to date, while any result above 1. 0 would indicate a cost underrun, in other words, we're below our budget. Let's look at an example. If we say that 55% of a $460, 000 project is complete, and that so far, the team has spent $257, 000, what would the current CPI be? At the current cost performance, would we expect the project to finish above or below our budgeted figure? 55% of $460, 000 is $253, 000. That would give us an earned value of $253, 000 given that 55% of our project work has been completed.

Compare that to our actual cost, and run that into our CPI formula, and you would see that we arrive at a CPI of roughly 0. 98. This would indicate that we're running slightly over budget compared to what our initial projected figures might have been. Schedule performance index is calculated in much the same way. It helps to answer the question of whether the project is running ahead or behind schedule based on its performance thus far. This formula is calculated as earned value divided by planned value, and any result below 1. 0 indicates that we have less work completed than we had initially planned, while any result above 1. 0 would indicate that more work is completed than planned. In this case, a project team is 40% done with its work after 7 months.

The project's deliverables must be completed in the next 8 months. What is the team's current SPI, and have they accomplished more or less than they expected? Well, if we see that they are 7 months into their current project and that the deliverables will be due in 8 months, that indicates a total duration for the project of 15 months. This gives us a present value of 7/15 or roughly 46. 67%. However, we only have an earned value of 40% to date. If we take these two figures, even without having any cost information available to us, we're able to calculate an SPI of. 857, which indicates that less work has been completed to date than would have been expected.

Finally, the burn rate answers the question of how quickly project funds are being depleted. This can be calculated in a variety of ways, but one of the best is the estimate to completion metric. This helps us understand how much more money is going to be required to get to the end of the project based on our performance to date. In this formula, ETC equals estimate to completion. BAC equals our budget at completion, or the total projected budget for the project. EV, once again, is earned value, and CPI is our cost performance index. Let's look at an example. A project has a budget of $10, 000. Thus far, $6, 000 worth of value have been created, but at a cost of $7, 500.

Assuming a similar level of cost overrun moving forward, what is our new estimated total cost for the project? First, we need to calculate our cost performance index by dividing our earned value by our actual cost. When we do so, we arrive at a figure of 0. 8. We can then calculate our estimate to completion by taking our initial budget of $10, 000 and subtracting the value of $6, 000 that's been created. This leaves us with $4, 000, which we then divide by our CPI figure of 0. 8. This indicates that our estimate to completion is $5, 000. This would also further indicate, based on an additional $5, 000 being necessary to finish project work, that our estimate at completion can be expected to be $12, 500 in total.

In other words, we should expect that the project will finish 25% above our initial project budget. By using these five key techniques, we're able to understand how our project is doing, both on a schedule and a cost basis, and ensure that the value we're creating is inline with our estimates and have the ability to make changes if necessary if we're not meeting that mark.

DEVELOPING A PROJECT'S BUDGET IS SIMILAR TO SCHEDULE

In many ways, developing a project's budget is similar to developing its schedule. That's appropriate given how closely the two are intertwined. A project that runs behind schedule is almost certain to experience cost overruns as well, and a project that isn't properly budgeted may experience delays related to funding, over expenditures, or resource constraints.

Developing our schedules and budgets side by side and ensuring that both stay updated as key project factors change over time is one of the most important roles that project managers undertake and one of those that's most central to project success. Earned value management techniques, in particular, offer us an opportunity to put a number on exactly how well we're doing and to see if changes in our funding might be necessary to keep project work running smoothly. With these new scheduling and budgeting skills in place, our focus will now shift to understanding and managing our project's communications needs and the various kinds of risks that can impact project success.

Those topics will be covered in the next Book in this series, Managing Project Communications and Risks, but for now, congratulations on completing this Book, improving your knowledge of project scheduling and budgeting best practices. And I'll hope to see you back here for the next Book as we continue to prepare for the CompTIA Project+ exam.